The Climb Back

Also by Pip Griffin and published by Pohutukawa Press
Salt Lake (2004)
Last song: the first year (2007)
Ani Lin: the journey of a Chinese Buddhist nun (2010)
*Margaret Caro: the extraordinary life of a pioneering dentist,
New Zealand 1848–1938: her story in verse*
(Highly Commended, Society of Women Writers NSW Book Awards 2020 – Poetry)
Envoi: Ted Rutter's selected poems 1990–2017 (2021, editor)
Virginia and Katherine: The Secret Diaries (2021)

By Pip Griffin with Colleen Keating
Mood Indigo (Picaro Poets, 2020)

Pip Griffin

The Climb Back

Poems for Ted

Acknowledgements

Some poems in this collection previously appeared in
Last Song: the first year, *Mood Indigo*, *Poetry Matters* and *Tamba*.

My very special thanks to Colleen Keating for invaluable critique,
editing, shaping and proofreading of the collection;
Mark Mahemoff for empathic appraisal and encouragement,
Ava Banerjee, Penelope Grace, Glenys Jackson, Paul Kane
and Jenny Stewart for their tributes and support;
John Griffin for his evocative cover design;
and the editors of Ginninderra Press for their encouragement
and dedication to publishing poetry.

The Climb Back: Poems for Ted
ISBN 978 1 76109 191 9
Copyright © text Pip Griffin 2021
Cover design: John Griffin

First published 2021 by
GINNINDERRA PRESS
PO Box 3461 Port Adelaide 5015
www.ginninderrapress.com.au

Contents

Beloved Place
  On firm sand   11
  Like crazy paving   12
  At the second meeting   13
  Writing lives   14
  To be (with you)   15
  Each other's way   16
  Coromandel Coast   17
  Pavane   18
  Life drawing   19
  Soft tent light   20
  Last song   21
  Trying to be Buddhist (about this)   22
  Every time we say goodbye…   23
  Devils' music   24
  Deep down   25
  On Piha Beach   26
  Little Golden Bay, Coromandel   28
  Papa Aroha again   29

Time Travelling
  This morning is of my imagining   33
  Day Street morning   34
  At Berkelouw's Café   35
  At Central Station   36
  Arran's Isle   37
  The church at Acaster Malbis   38
  Stansted Express   39
  Eurostar to Paris   40
  Swimming among crocodiles   41

Waiting for a flight	43
Manchester to Singapore	44
Time travelling	45

Wild Places

Leonard Cohen was a brave man	49
Your father's house	50
Water music	51
Ted at DCR	52
While he's away	54
And I will keep	55
Birthday poem	56
Spirits Bay	57
That day	58
Chameleon Man	59
The climb back	60

Nearly August

The Table at the Umu Café	63
Nearly August	65
More than most men	66
Isfahan	67
Jupiter	68
Departures	69
Leura Gardens	71
Palm Beach	72
Sixteen months on	73
Old dressing gown	74
Dressed in style	75
Coast walking	76

There will come a day

Loch Lomond	79
Genesis	81

Jupiter again	82
Inquisitive angels	83
St Valentine's Day poems	84
Travelling alone	86
April	88
Outside my bedroom window	89
There will come a day	90
Notes	91

What we have once enjoyed we can never lose,
for all we deeply love becomes a part of us.
– Helen Keller

In all our searching, the only thing we have ever found
that makes the emptiness bearable is each other.
– Carl Sagan

Beloved Place

On firm sand

near Papa Aroha*
my shoes settle
among the delicate prints
of oystercatchers
that peck at
seaweed
crabs
sandhoppers
shells

I am Gulliver
on this shore
watching their long bills
red as sunsets
work in unison
with lapping waves.

* Papa Aroha – love of place, love of the land, beloved place; coastal village on the Coromandel Peninsula, NZ

Like crazy paving

That moment you flung yourself
into my present
our future stretched like crazy paving

the possible stark-lit in black and white
its danger flashes sharp as jagged glass
irresistible as blood-pink sundew

yet rainbowed with delight
love, laughter
a kind of happiness allowed

a hope of breaking patterns
surviving pain

a hope that maybe this time
we'd get it right.

At the second meeting

you shared your words

not read

said

and I'd been worrying
what I'd say if they
were second-rate

yet your voice (your lovely voice)
spoke lines of love

made pictures for me

an intimation
of what could come

of what

could be.

Writing lives

If we could write our lives in poetry
and strew the way with naught but sheer delights
would nightmares take us riding in the dark
or dreams of astral flying fill our nights

if we could live on words   together be
would bed and books and dictionary sustain
keep us loving and in tune
for any years of life which might remain

if we could try to often speak with truth
and live with love in utmost honesty
we might be good together you and I –
could write our lives in one eternity.

To be (with you)

Like a poem's birth struggle
this ache
yearns
pulses
clamours
claws
pushes where skin is thinnest

demands break-out
will crawl
walk
run
swim
fly
any thing

brave sea-miles
wind
hail
snow
storm
mountain
to be
(with you)

covenanting
some thing
surrendering
no thing
giving
every thing.

Each other's way

Remember fears
of how we'd live
small scale
cramped
in each other's way

would irritations shadow
love's bright eyes
and dull the dreams

seems fears were groundless, dear
we move with care
in gentle dance

being in each other's
way's no hardship

if we could climb
into each other's skins
we would.

Coromandel Coast

Name
once a part
of childhood's fantasies

khaki shorts
sola tepees

jungle fastnesses
the loneliness of sand

heat
drums
romance

Place
more gorgeous
than desire

the landscape
proffers wairua ora*

hills
islands
sea

a beauty
real as my beloved's body

as difficult to leave.

* wairua ora – satisfied spirit

Pavane

Above the Binney hills
the seabirds' flight

cascading rain streaks
columns grey and white

the gull that gulped
our bread has flown

and parents drag
reluctant children home

thinking sunshine here
has had its day

though still it shines
on our side of the bay

where we in silence
satisfied, replete

watch waves in slow pavane
advance, retreat…

Life drawing

Draw her
draw him

use
soft willow

tilt forms
each
to other

have them
touch

dance them
in negative
space

edge them
with light

give them
murmured shadows

a notion
of perfection

the possibility
of happiness.

Soft tent light

My country now his
my memories lie
acquiescent
in soft tent light
past beckoning
with fern-frond fingers

pohutukawa* blaze
hills' rough green corduroy
imprinted sixty years ago

his memories lie
skin-close
close to tears

graves found
not found
days made oblivious
by children's mud-filled play
the floating world's explosion
propelling him past boundaries
impelling him to write
the universe

my memories swim
on love's charged surface
tumble in the breakers
of his sea

sink
in soft tent light.

* pohutukawa – *Metrosideros excelsa* – New Zealand Christmas tree

Last song

(after Richard Strauss)

I'll tell you
how a last soul-song is sung

so far from life's safe modulations
structured harmonies

as bodies soften with old melodies
and tentative duets begin anew

I wonder   can the notes sustain

will this song be the last –
the one sung here with you?

Trying to be Buddhist (about this)

It's hard being Buddhist
trying to live the present moment
when you live in me

I breathe in peace
and breathe out joy
and you are joy

I conjure white light
confuse spiritual with carnal

ask for help

it's difficult to do this
being Buddhist.

Every time we say goodbye...

This morning, over sea-miles

        you sang for me

we know this song

        know major becomes minor

emotions see-sawing

        from threnody to jubilate

lives as different in their scoring

        as Palestrina from Prokofiev

recapitulated separations

        playing us shrill

reunions – impossibly –

        an epithalamium.

Devils' music

There's danger in the dream
the manufactured
transmuted into tangible

dreamers invent reality
ignore forebodings
see only rainbows
and perfect waves

while co-grouped atoms bounce
an intimation of existence
chemicals play nervous
systems with taut bows

make devils' music
we're too blind to hear.

With shut eyes open wide
we live each other's dream.

Deep down

the vigilant hobgoblins
are hard at it

searching for evidence
carefully noting any
hint of shadow
uneven surface
weak point
hairline crack
widening fissure

editing, annotating
nodding recognition
passing judgement
smug
secure
swollen with self-righteousness
pumped with power

their job to undermine

they have lists

they expect (to have)
the last
word.

On Piha Beach

As we drive
down
through the Waitakeres

past fern tunnels
to the hidden places
where the wealthy
lived my dreams

a shrouded image
from my memory
scrabbles to the light

that's it!
the wife-to-be
slept with her husband's best man
on the night before the wedding

how I'd envied her and her fiancé
their sophistication
edgy sexuality
smug knowingness

I'd envied her bravado –
to do that thing
to risk
still being loved

after the marriage
they'd lived near Titirangi
before decamping to Australia
brown land of opportunity

down on Piha Beach
as you and I
walk a stretch of black-shot
shell-strewn sand

a young woman
turns her head
to smile at me.

Little Golden Bay, Coromandel

On this small
stony beach
h-rurrrush   h-rurrrush
of waves
evokes a childhood
East Coast expedition

my parents
and a caravan
of floating each night
into sea dreams
waking
to sea music

the sound brings
extraordinary ease
an almost happiness
a knowing
that all's in its place
as perfect now
as it will ever be.

Papa Aroha again

Sun's hot on my body
sea's susurrus just audible
the bay close
so close that if you were to cross the tar-sealed road
you'd see through pohutukawas' entwined arms
the waves' inexorable advance   retreat
the pair of oystercatchers sift through shells
the heron's stilt-walk in a shallow rock pool
the shags open their sodden wings like flashers' raincoats
the gannet rise in smooth, perfect trajectory.

Once on this beach
I was as alien as Gulliver
my giant footprints sullying the shore.
Today I wish, like Gilgamesh,
to be forever in this moment
to float on tuis'* four-note carillons over blue-green islands
to ride with mares' tails across the Coromandel sky.

* tui – parson bird

Time Travelling

This morning is of my imagining

This morning is of my imagining
in years of weekend mornings spent alone

observing couples share a café table
newspaper looks conversation touch

I imagined mornings with a lover –
peaceful in shared   unhurried   timeless space

this morning you spoke aloud what I was thinking –
this morning we are doing it, my love.

Day Street morning

In this one moment
with loved one's absence lying
mute on right side of my bed
there's the inevitable aircraft
barking of a neighbour's dog
swish swish of motor on the road

beyond my window
robot hum of Marion Street buses
the wattlebird on my grevillea
squawk squawking spring
some sad distant dove
calling for its mate

in this one moment
a magpie's quardle ardle oodle
sings to me of ecstasy
a pure and joyful temple bell
a chant of love.

At Berkelouw's Café

At Berkelouw's Café   bereft
········words come
now you have left

I read your Robin Hood's Bay poem
········its brilliance once more
catching my breath

flying me to where you and I
········climbed ruined castle walls
breathed ancient air

sat side by side
········on heathered brae
walked childhood's way

on Whitby's sunset sands
········Filey's fine shore
and followed North Sea cliffs
········to where the gannets flew

we could have walked on water then
········with all we knew.

At Central Station

After our early morning phone call plans
I'm here again at Central Station
by brick wall
in winter sunlight
with too-hot coffee

across from a young woman
whose bare dirty feet splay
as she sleeps up against sandstone façade
and railway employees smoke
their morning tea break

and I see you and me
travelling in England
our fears admitted
dealt to   dealt with
optimism soaring
in delicious anticipation of
another month together

our romance held high
in jubilation.

Arran's Isle

While walking Castle Brodick's halls
did I expect to feel familial ghosts' breath cold upon my skin

the shades of ancestors to show as light in corners of my vision
the painted eyes of some gaunt Hamilton to follow me
around a room?

We'd seen haphazard graves in feral disarray
among the wildflowers and the weeds near Goatfell's path

their dull inscriptions whispering the time-eroded names of
long-dead dukes.

There was a moment when we'd walked through
verdigris-bronze-purple
to a burn that cadenced to the indigo of Breadhaig harbour

(the village spilled there and the ferries trailed their spume
across to Ardrossan)

when we sat half-hidden in harsh arcs of heather
as a golden eagle soared and swooped for us alone –

there was a moment when I felt my forbears gathered close
behind me.

The church at Acaster Malbis

A second coming

Yorkshire fields in autumn mode
churchyard new-mown
fresh painted gate   green-lichened stones

constant   vouchsafed
deep-rooted in tranquillity
unlock with antiquated key
this mystery's Holy Trinity

here lies Stone Knight on cold stone slab
white form rubbed smooth
by generations of the faithful's hands

now breathe in pious, entombed air
breathe atoms of six hundred years

all disbelief ends here.

Stansted Express

We travel
on a silent train
to nowhere
track both sides for miles
a dump for dead machines
– graffiti heaven.

You remember
black dog London winters
when your spirit
travelled nowhere.

This train connects me
with the need
to do this Europe thing without you –
your early morning imprints
still pressed into my skin.

Again we'll break our physical connection
our journey aberrated
to breath's length.

You'll travel back to family
I on – to do the second bravest thing
I've ever done.

Eurostar to Paris

This time
you're left in London
with our baggage
to be transported
with some difficulty
to East Dulwich

while I'm excited
aboard at last –
a seat alone
first carriage
in hushed, smooth-swaying glide
through backyard Britain

left with your touch
kiss
words
reiterating tomorrow's rendezvous

this thirty-six hours
without each other
but a sneeze
amongst all separations
we endure.

Swimming among crocodiles

There

the waterhole is
red-rock fringed
lushly foliaged

dark

still

deep

irresistible
after hours spine-jaggling
in the troop carrier

there's even a friendly waterfall
to play with.

They tell us there are freshies here
but they'll be frightened more of us
than we of them.

I know there's jeopardy
within the poetry
you've brought me

and fear
insidious in its rising
from belly
into chest

throat

mouth.

The mastering of this
will take me
far beyond
an ordinary fear

of swimming among crocodiles.

Waiting for a flight

Waiting
for a flight
delayed by floods

I watch a dozen Virgin aircraft
taxi through pinpoints
of pulsing lights

rise into late afternoon sky
over low pale buildings

their grey-pink windows
delicate as rice paper screens.

When we meet
after months of paper-feelings
paper-thoughts

will our mouths
be able to form words?

I cannot see
beyond two images:

you emerging from Arrivals

shaving in my bathroom.

Cannot feel beyond
the holding of each other

and the quieting of fear.

Manchester to Singapore

You're deep in *JFK* the movie
we've hardly touched
or spoken for two hours

in boredom's bondage
bubble-wrapped
bookless, pen, paperless

I move
stretch
eat a chocolate

at last
you ask the girl with almond eyes
for pens and paper.

They save us
from ourselves.

Time travelling

20 ks out from Opotiki
it's as if the countryside
has concertinaed

green hedges
white sheep
beige cows
well behaved remnant native forest

landscape neat
as a child's toy farm

maybe we're time travellers
perhaps it's a parallel universe

or has love encapsulated reality
changed perception
slowed heartbeats

placed us in
the palm of its hand.

Wild Places

Leonard Cohen was a brave man

Showed yourself to me half-opened
lives laid bare though not completely

wisdom sweated from a fire box
novice turn about with teacher

glowing gifts for me to carry
packages of hard-learnt lessons

dreamed that night a day together
friendship, closeness, joy of living

whither from this place of beauty
muted roar of waves on shoreline

tui calls in remnant forest
whither with my solitude?

Your father's house

Alone
I light a candle
for where it's morning
in your father's house

you've been burning candles
for life
for death
for memory
for love
alone inside your father's house
soul's intimation whispering
it is not yet time

candles to ease him out
as once they eased you in

my flame is almost candle's length
and steady
flaring dark places
singing to the edges of reality.

Water music

You once told me that when a boy
your first paid job was tending rowing boats
on the River Ouse.

I see you – eager, nervous
meticulous in carrying out your tasks:
cleaning, rowing, mooring.

You rowed us on the lake in Pukekura Park
and again in ancient Knaresborough
where a viaduct bestrides the River Nidd.

The to-and-fro of your arms made water music.
I was mesmerised by the rhythm
your far-away gaze, the shape of your mouth.

Afterwards we drank coffee at the riverside tearoom
as the warmth of the day haloed us with love
and the river mirrored our happiness.

Ted at DCR

By seven on a workday morning
he's grateful for the solitude
skipping down two hundred steps
no fear of falling (he likes falling!)
hearing the soft thwack of his boots on stone
a tui[1] (first to rise) trilling above his head.

A poem tests its fledgling wings.

He stops to chat with two piwakawaka[2]
(his little darlings) that flicker flutter
peck dart swoop amongst white-starred
bee-busy kanuka[3]
breathes soul-soothing aromas:
primordial damp earth
moss flower plant tree.

A cicada choir confirms it's summer.

He pauses to greet the kauri[4]
its orange/red/brown kiri-plates[5]
rougher than his work-tough hands
that caress trailing rimu[6] fronds
release some branches that crave freedom
salute the terracotta sculptures sentinel in early sun.

Now below him there are sounds:
coughs
grunts
the odd word
laughter
hammer taps on wood
clash of steel on steel
the rumble of a kiln (he smells its smoke)
the train engine's grumbling start-up.

His other world begins.

1. tui – parson bird
2. piwakawaka – fantail
3. kanuka – *Kunzea ericoides*
4. kauri – *Agathis australis* – black pine
5. kiri – bark, literally skin
6. rimu – red pine

While he's away

go to some marvellous place
within yourself she said
when I was voicing fears
and lack of trust
that you'd return
from spirit's pilgrimage

so I've been trying

and every time the longing comes
the need to touch
to know you still exist
I concentrate on images of your emergence
from that beautiful wild place

on hearing your beloved voice

but that secured
there's more to overcome
you have another grail
a quest for resolution

it's right –
renew connections
lay history's persistent ghosts
now if you will

return strong hearted

we two still have
some things here
we need to do

And I will keep

in heart and mind

a vision of your emergence

not like butterfly from chrysalis

but as a hawk

sky-dancing

in upward trajectory

released from Manapouri's arms

Birthday poem

Today
you rang me
– unexpectedly –
declared your love
said I'd changed your life

said that tomorrow
you'll change your will
leave all your poems to me

today I say:
a poet has no greater love
than this

he leaves
his poetry
to me.

Spirits Bay

You come to the house

you come to the house made secret
by pohutukawas' ancient magic
their labyrinthine protection

you come to the house made sensuous
by rimus' flowing arms
where sunsets illuminate each room
where susurrus of sea enters your dreams

you come to the house which in every storm
will carry you from crest to crest
as you live its rhythm
as you take its centre to be yours
as you accept its gift

knowing it is the place from where to soar.

That day

he had (she said)
that day
eyes for you only

my eyes saw eagerness –
the hard-edged energy
of older men whose sexuality
still leaps and flares around their bodies
like sun's fire

that day
attracted by the heat
I trusted the sharp punch to the gut

the vision blazing in the mind's eye.

Chameleon Man

How many facets of you are there?
How many separate personalities in one?
Not only does your face change –
your demeanour, your reactions, your behaviour

to name some of the surprising ways
you metamorphose
a guru then a novice, old to young.
I think I've seen you all, then of a sudden
manifestation new replaces known.

You say we know each other better
through illness – shared, matured
while coping with its run
but
don't stop chameleoning, love, amaze me!
Keep metamorphosing in the years to come.

The climb back

With unexpected kauri
near leaf-littered track
terrain soft-cushioned
journey swift

no turning back

no grasping tree roots
no green moss-slicked stone
this path
this way
so right

he's coming home

through tears
in opaque canopy of self-pitched night
a glimpse of unity
of radiant light

soul-kite's taut string released
from earth's frail grasp
this climb's back to eternity

his place

at last.

Nearly August

The Table at the Umu Café

Fourteen years ago today
heart in overdrive
I went to meet you

you were seated
apparently composed
but just as quaky
at the table that became The Table

I was captivated when you read
your poems to me at DCR
you'd met every down-train for a week
hoping I'd keep my promise

we exchanged poetry books
voiced no plans
but there was no turning back
desire took us both prisoner

at the Table we talked
ate
you drank wine
I appraised you

strong arms
workman's hands
sensual mouth
slight Yorkshire accent

you told me much about your past
your work
your women
children

that you loved Walt Whitman
and Leonard Cohen
birds
my poetry

the hobgoblins were about
checking off their lists
you talked too much about yourself
shared information
I thought too intimate for a first date

were so intense I thought
you'd overwhelm me
gobble my independence

I ignored the voices
and wrote two poems that night
first of a plethora that followed.

Nearly August

These balmy days have set me weeping
the same warmth that so delighted us
when we, eager, jittery, impelled
first leapt into our love

these days hold memories of all our autumn walks
the gardens where we breathed manuka, boronia and rose
the essence of the landscapes
their sensual warmth again, here, now

I gathered white camellias to put beside you
in the long days of your dying
clouds of native flowers lay on your coffin

August marks your coming and your going
and our fair and cloudless days.

More than most men

Thinking of the words you've left
('more than most men' she wrote to me)
yet needing today to read others' poetry
I choose *prayers of a secular world*
find you in so many – these delicate formations:
a dying father's handshake with a son
birds, our modern angels, singing day's break to day's end
sharing love with perfect promiscuity
two nuns in silent, beneficent communion, peeling pears
a daughter's visit to her dead father's tool shed, evoking your gaze
at Bunnings' shelves of nails, screws, bolts
devout as any monk en-trance in solitary cell and every bit as sacred
the red candle's brave and steady flame
perfection of beach pebbles
a plain stone in a cemetery
small garden's thriving beans and brassicas
certain music
the murmuring of trees
relentless ratcheting of jet planes over Leichhardt roofs
all instances of you about and visiting me.

Isfahan

You spoke of Isfahan –
its name soughing
heat, sand, white

robes and poetry.
In *Half the World*
a city of your odyssey

you came upon the
Great Bazaar where
*tajirs** beguiled you

with their carpets –
wondrous-patterned
gloriously hued –

bewitched you with their woven stories.
You desired a *kilim*†
but could not take it with you

Isfahan to be forever linked
with longing for its mystery
and the people's open hearts.

* *tajirs* – traders, merchants
† *kilim* – carpet

Jupiter

I heard Holst's 'Jupiter' today
surprised that I could listen without crying
to the music you so loved

I asked that it be played
as they carried your coffin
from the Anglican Church Hall

being deaf with grief
I have no memory of the music.

Departures

Having largely forgotten
the detail of the film
but remembering that you loved it
as did I, for its humanity
its gentleness
its delicate depiction of an occupation
that many, now so detached from death
will stigmatise as gruesome
somewhat grotesque –
the preparation of dead bodies
for burning or burial –
I was brutally confronted by families
watching the ritual cleansings
of their dead.

We were alone in your last hours.
I sang hoping (knowing) you could hear me.
Watched the cancer's unstoppable trajectory
until the moment that it drowned you.

I held your hand.
The doctor came and went.
Two nurses helped me wash, shave
dress you.

I watched the undertaker cocoon you.
Take you from me.

At your funeral the wildflower-covered coffin
that I chose was closed.
How did I know that you were in it?

Forgive me, dear, for not accompanying you
on your last, long, Thames Coast drive.
I never wanted you to be alone.

Leura Gardens

While travelling by train to this place we visited so often
a reservoir of tears presses against my ribs

i do not want this pain to fill
the hollow of your absence

images of our time together explode behind my eyes
'The Lark Ascending' plays to my inner ear

cherry trees in blossom line the streets
like flower girls at a wedding

the gardens flaunt their colours
I wear the striped jumper we bought here

at the Waldorf Gardens Resort
a jazz group plays 'Mood Indigo' under the spent wisteria.

Palm Beach

Gale-driven waves slap
        bronze sand.
Surfers – biding their time –
        bob like black seals.

They lay close here
        on a grassy slope
now devoured by real estate.

He read to her
        from his 'rough books'
brought from Coromandel.

One poem outraged her –
        how could he allow
a past passion to intrude upon
        their fledgling love?

Driven to share his poetry
        he did not notice her distress
until she voiced it.
        He was bewildered.

Years later
        when she met the woman
she found no rival

yet when he was dying
        watching her sit close
to him and stroke his leg
        she felt again that Palm Beach pang.

Sixteen months on

and at my daughter's house
> it's clear, hot Christmas.

Diamonds of latticework
> pattern bare floorboards.

In a breeze as gentle as a lover's hand
> shadows of palm fronds swish their skirts.

A boy's eighteen today. Too soon a man –
> he may sleep on till noon.

And you, my dearest, loom next to me
> benign shade of past Christmases

together in so many places   so many
> it is unthinkable I'll ever not remember.

Old dressing gown

Your faithful, rather ragged dressing gown
which you could not give up
after buying the new blue fleece

is now my comforter
becoming mine as easily
as I wrapped it around me in your little house.

It was an extra blanket
on coldest Coromandel nights
when the warmth of our bodies was not enough.

Sometimes I spread it on my winter bed
which will never again know
the comfort of your body next to mine.

Dressed in style

Today I was reminded
that two months before the diagnosis
you, most frugal of men

splurged –
bought some 'quality' clothes
a final indulgence

in the hospice
when not in your comfortable dressing gown
you were dressed in style

and at the end, although no one would see
I chose your favourite polo-neck and jeans
for your ultimate adornment.

Coast walking

Today
you're with me
as I walk the clifftop way
its turf muddied
by marauding canines

yet – amongst the despoliation
I see your familiars

two willy wagtails – close cousins of your piwakawaka
alight upon a picket fence
and dance for me

welcome swallows
swoop close like paper planes
hurled by excited schoolboys

and far below spray shoots upward –
like waves pound the Thames Coast
in a Coromandel storm.

# There will come a day

Loch Lomond

1

Nicola Benedetti's on Classic FM
        her joyous violin playing
songs of her homeland
        that take me back to Scotland.

While we drove you sang every Scottish song
        you ever knew
brave baritone enhanced
        by the soft brogue you did so well.

The afternoon we came upon the Loch
        your monsters lay quiescent
as you scanned the waters –
        wide open to the metaphysical

to the occult
        to ancient magic
hoping Nessie
        would reveal herself that day.

2

With you at tether's end
        at last we saw a signpost
to a B&B.

A darkly winding road.
        Our host, alone in gothic
many-bedroomed house

served us venison for dinner.
        That night we got no sleep –
the drumming! as if the ghosts

of sad Culloden's Field
        re-sounded their inglorious retreat
to terrorise the tourists.

At breakfast our good host explained
        it was the New Age worshippers
calling up Cailleachan

said to drift in eldritch loch night mists.
        Damned nuisance, he said.
They do it every year.

Genesis

William Robinson's paintings
have come to Sydney
from the north
        where you were happy

delighting in the warm days
tropical gardens
ferry rides
        our river walks

the South Bank's strings of galleries
the restaurants –
even the ersatz beach
        delighted you.

Near the Botanic Gardens we entered
the old Governor's Residence
its sandstone inner sanctum
        another Eden

a triptych dome
with Turner skies
transfigured landscape
        painted with a god's gaze.

Here was the drama of your vision
multidimensioned
palpable
        apparent to your third eye.

Jupiter again

Today I listen to Holst's 'Jupiter' with joy.

I've come to love your funeral processional

the quasi-anthem

its triumphal march.

Today it thrills me and uplifts me

and I know that you are waiting

deep within the greatest anthem

at one with the soundlessness of the cosmos.

Inquisitive angels

If indeed there is a god
I know she'll let you
ride your rig around Valhalla

inquisitive young angels
will gather
admire it

they'll ask, 'Why is the
sidecar empty, Ted?'
and you'll say, 'She couldn't
come with me on my last ride.'

St Valentine's Day poems

Let us live in such a way
That when we die
Our love will survive
And continue to grow.
The Prayer Tree – Michael Leunig

1. Protective cloak

Your love is a kahu-feather cloak*
protective
weatherproof, soft, warm
so soft
so very warm.
I wrap it around myself
in times of need.

2. Romance

Because of your romantic nature
we marked St Valentine's Day
with cards
a special dinner if we were together
or, if not, you sent me flowers
until the tribulations of their arrival
outweighed their symbolism.

3. Flowers

When I arrived at Auckland Airport
you always gave me flowers.

You waited patiently
wearing shorts in summer
your jeans in winter
holding your modest offerings.

4. The colour red

For your 70th birthday I sent a dozen roses, red
by InterFlora, to Driving Creek Railway.
At dinner we always lit a red candle.
This St Valentine's Day I'll light one
for remembrance.

* kahu – hawk

Travelling alone

In the familiar apartment
the bed expects to feel
the heft of him beside her

the sheets to bear
the imprint of his body
next to hers.

She's rediscovering
the uncertain pleasures
of travelling alone

talks with him as she walks
through man-created rainforest
to the imitation beach

talks to a butcher-bird
that perches very close to her
on a riverside park bench

watches people
on electric scooters
skilfully avoid the walkers.

She misses
their remembering
for each other.

He would not have let her
nearly leave her suitcase
on the platform

would have remembered how to find
the Robinson Gallery
amongst the hodgepodge buildings

would have shared her muffin
with their decaf coffees
at the QUT café.

Yet alone she finds
she can still enjoy
the paintings as intensely

feel the wonder that he felt
as if he still stood gazing
at her side

talk to the friendly custodian
without his exuberance
overshadowing   overwhelming

sit quietly
in the rose gardens
they loved so much

feel comfortable alone –
yet long for him who gave
travel its piquancy.

April

Today
the Bay's perfect aqua peace
mirrors the April when we met

both leading solitary lives
believing love had forgotten us
when it proffered its gift

and bathed us in beneficence
to match those balmy
blue-green Coromandel days.

Outside my bedroom window

Outside my bedroom window
a sleek red wattlebird
quaffs from grevillea flowers

could it be the very one that sang for joy
those spring mornings
when you were here?

There will come a day

There will come a day when you will think about him and smile before you cry. (Attributed to Joe Biden)

I read the phrase a week ago
and, as always
when synchronicity occurs
I heard it again yesterday
in the movie *Hearts and Bones*.

I know it's happening to me

In the third year since your death
I can often (but not always)
think of you and smile
remembering our happiness and our love
before tears come.

Notes

'Pavane' – Don Binney (1940–2012), NZ artist famous for paintings of birds in the landscape.

'On Piha Beach' – All north of Auckland, NZ: Piha Beach, Waitakeres (mountain range), Titirangi (suburb).

'Papa Aroha again' – *The Epic of Gilgamesh* (King of Uruk, Mesopotamia), describes the existential struggles of a man who must reconcile himself to his mortality and find meaning in his life despite the inevitability of death. Written about 1800 BC, it is thought to be one of the earliest surviving examples of epic poetry.

'Day Street Morning' – Denis Glover poem, 'The Magpies'.

'At Berkelouw's Café' – Robin Hood's Bay, Whitby and Filey are all coastal towns in North Yorkshire, UK.

'Time Travelling' – Opotiki: town in eastern Bay of Plenty, North Island, NZ.

'Water Music' – Pukekura Park, New Plymouth, NZ.
River Ouse, York & Knaresborough, Yorkshire, UK.

'Ted at DCR' – DCR: Driving Creek Railway & Pottery, Coromandel Town, NZ.

'And I will keep' – Lake Manapouri, South Island, NZ.

'Spirits Bay' – Te Rerenga Wairua: Spirits' leaping-off place, Cape Reinga, north-western-most tip of the North Island, NZ.

'More than most men' – This poem contains references to poems in 'Delicate formation of faults', a subsection of the anthology *Prayers of a Secular World*, Inkerman & Blunt, 2015, eds Jordie Albiston & Kevin Brophy; Leichhardt: inner-west suburb of Sydney, Australia.

'Isfahan' – *Isfahan nasf-e jahan*, 'Isfahan is half the world', was an ancient name for the city.

'Departures' – *Departures*: a Japanese film about a young man who returns to his hometown after a failed career as a cellist and stumbles across work as a *nokanshi* – a traditional Japanese ritual mortician.

'Loch Lomond' – *cailleachan*: Celtic spirits.

'Genesis' – William Robinson, *Creation Landscape: The Dome of Space and Time* (2003–4).

'Travelling Alone' – The William Robinson Gallery in Old Government House, Queensland University of Technology, Australia.

www.ingramcontent.com/pod-product-compliance
Lightning Source LLC
Chambersburg PA
CBHW062139100526
44589CB00014B/1627